The Space Between

Heidy Lozano

BookLeaf Publishing

India | USA | UK

Presentation by *BookLeaf Publishing*

Web: www.bookleafpub.com

E-mail: info@bookleafpub.com

ISBN: 9789363317703

First edition 2024

To Maggie. My best friend, soulmate and love of my life. My life will never be the same without you. Thank you for rescuing me. Forever my best girl.

Paper thin cuts

The ache never subsided.
It hid somewhere deep in the crevices of my
heart where it took a life of it's own.
I danced around with a smile on my face but the
truth was invisible to those around me.
Most days it was invisible even to me, but when
I sat quietly enough, I could feel the paper thin
cuts to the heart.
The ache never subsided but I had to move on.
Because how do I live without pressing play
even though the mistake was mine.

I'll wait

I sat in a corner and waited.
I waited my turn to feel again.
I waited for the numbness to escape my body.
But,It didn't come.
The emptiness didn't abate.
It's more vast, it's more profound.
But here, in the same corner.
I'll wait.

Be there again

I want to be back there again.
Before knowing what I know now.
Living in that moment.
I want to change the outcome of a few things.
I want to live a mundane routine and soak up
every minute of it.
I want to be there again and love you again.

Take me back

I'd like to turn back time.
I'd like to live the moments I forgot to live.
I'd like to be present when I thought I wanted to leave.
I want to sit in dad's lap again and feel weightless.
I want to watch my sister dress up and dream of being her when I grow older.
I want to hold my mom's hand while she shops and enjoy every second of it.
I want to ride in the car with my brother and sing along to our favorite songs.
Take me back to a time before I wanted to grow up.
I didn't know I never actually wanted to grow up.

Maggie

I walked into a room with 60 more just like you.
Suddenly all eyes were on me and I couldn't
move.
When I got near all the noise disappeared, it was
just you and me.
I knew right then we were meant to be.
My life began on a beautiful autumn evening
when you chose me.
I will live every day to love you and care for
you.
You saved my life, now it's time for me to save
yours.
When it's time for us to move on from each
other (because life isn't eternal)
Just know, you completed me like a puzzle piece
from heaven.
I will love you always and forget you never.
Forever my soulmate you'll be.

Helen

In the comfort of your living room, just us girls,
We'd share moments, watching movies unfurl.
Your favorite tales spoke of journeys afar,
Traveling the world, under sun and star.

Lessons you taught, engraved in my heart,
To seize each day, to love every part.
Spring and fall in Tacoma, a cherished retreat,
In your presence, life felt complete.

Your quirks, your laughter, your zest for life,
Each moment with you, a treasure rife.
But most of all, your joy in the mundane,
Taught me to dance in the gentle rain.

Grandma dear, your spirit ever bright,
Guides me through the darkest night.
In your embrace, I find solace and grace,
Forever cherished, in your love's embrace.

Do over

Consider starting over.
Consider romanticizing every moment.
Consider keeping a diary and taking constant pictures.
Consider reliving every moment like it's your last.
Consider how you would love knowing it's the last time.
I would do it over.
I would love you again and do it better.
I would recreate every memory to submerge myself in it.
I would do it right this time and this time, I wouldn't let go.

Forget

Forget me please.
Forget the way I loved you.
Forget the way I made you laugh.
Forget the way I touched you and made you feel.
Forget me please, I can't go on like this.
Forget that we were meant to be.
Forget that I lived to make you smile.
But please never forget, my soul belongs to you.

My Girl

I can still hear your tiny paws racing to the room
at first light.
I can feel your warm breath on my pillow.
I looked forward to your cuddles every morning.
I never knew how much I needed you until that
first morning you woke up next to my bedside.
I knew I wanted you, but I didn't know you
would cure me of all the loneliness I had once
felt.
Some days were hard, some days were stressful
but every single day was fun and I felt loved.
And now, towards the end I am only grateful for
every moment we spent.
I would do anything to turn back time and do it
all over again.
Just you and me.
Forever my soulmate you'll be.

My best girl

You are my best friend.
You've seen me through every stage of my
adulthood.
You've seen me laugh and cry.
You've been with me through partners and
friends.
You've met every person I have loved.
And you've managed to love them just as much
as I do.
You didn't meet a friend of mine you didn't love.
I will forever cherish every moment we shared.
Don't go too far, I'll come meet you where you
are.
Forever my best girl.

Big girl

I woke up this morning and you were gone.
I knew you wouldn't be there but I woke up anyway.
10 years of waking up at the crack of dawn to feed you, to cuddle with you.
How will I move on from this emptiness you left.
How do I undo 10 years worth of habits and routines.
I knew this would hurt, but you took a piece of me I can never gain back.

My Twins

In the quiet realm where dreams take flight,
Twins yet unborn, bathed in soft moonlight.
Two souls entwined, in love's tender embrace,
Await their moment, in time and space.

In your gentle whispers, they hear your voice,
Guiding them onward, their hearts rejoice.
With each passing day, they grow and thrive,
In the sacred dance of life's sweet drive.

Through laughter and tears, they'll learn and
grow,
Bound by a love only parents can bestow.
With each step they take, they'll light the way,
Two stars in the sky, come what may.

So cherish this journey, both near and far,
For your twins, dear parent, are the brightest
star.
In their eyes, find hope, in their hearts, find
grace,
For they are the promise of tomorrow's embrace.

Timing

In the tapestry of time, love is spun,
By the hands of fate, by the rays of the sun.
In the gentle whisper of God's divine,
Love blooms, in His perfect design.

Through moments of joy, and trials untold,
Love's story unfolds, in hues bold.
For in God's timing, love's purest rhyme,
We find solace, in His sacred chime.

In every heartbeat, in every breath,
Love's essence lingers, conquering death.
For in the dance of eternity's reel,
God's love shines, in a love so real.

So trust in His timing, in every turn,
For in His love, we forever yearn.
In the rhythm of life, in God's grand scheme,
Love's melody plays, like a timeless dream.

Healing Time

In the labyrinth of anguish, where shadows
roam,
Time strides forth, weaving tales of its own.
With each passing moment, a healing balm,
A gentle touch, a soothing calm.

Through the darkest nights, and the brightest
days,
Time whispers softly, in mysterious ways.
It heals the wounds that once ran deep,
Guiding souls from sorrow to sleep.

Though pain may linger, like a haunting ghost,
Time's tender embrace becomes the host.
It teaches patience, it teaches grace,
Turning scars into lines of embrace.

So let time's gentle hand, its magic weave,
In its embrace, find solace, believe.
For in the passage of moments, we find release,
Curing pain with time, a gift of peace.

Wanderlust love

In the heart of wanderlust, love takes flight,
On wings of adventure, in the still of the night.
Through valleys deep and mountains high,
Love's flame burns bright, beneath the sky.

In foreign lands and distant shores,
Love's journey beckons, forevermore.
Hand in hand, souls intertwined,
Exploring the world, with love as the guide.

Through bustling streets and quiet lanes,
Love's whispers echo, amidst the rains.
In every corner, in every embrace,
Wanderlust and love, find their place.

For in the dance of exploration's spree,
Love's sweet melody sets us free.
In the embrace of the unknown's allure,
Wanderlust and love, forever endure.

Lovers dance

In the moonlit ballroom, where dreams take
flight,
Two hearts entwined, beneath the softest light.
With every step, a whispered sigh,
As they dance together, under the starry sky.

In the rhythm of the music's embrace,
They sway and twirl, in a lover's grace.
Lost in the moment, lost in the trance,
Their souls united, in a passionate dance.

Their bodies move as one, in perfect sync,
As they spin and dip, on the brink.
Of a love so pure, a love so true,
In each other's arms, they find their view.

For in the dance of romance's hold,
Their love story unfolds, bold and untold.
In the tender embrace of the night's romance,
They find eternal bliss, in the dance.

Father's love

In the shelter of his arms, I find my peace,
A love so pure, that will never cease.
Like a beacon in the night, his love shines
bright,
Guiding me through darkness, with its gentle
light.

In his unwavering gaze, I see grace unfold,
A love so deep, a story untold.
With every word, a whisper of divine,
In his love, I find solace, in every line.

Like the steady hand of a guiding force,
His love mirrors God's, on its eternal course.
In every sacrifice, in every prayer,
His love reflects God's, beyond compare.

For in the heart of a father's embrace,
I feel the warmth of God's own grace.
In his love, I see a glimpse of heaven above,
For a father's love, mirrors God's endless love.

My sister

In the merry dance of life's delight,
Two sisters twirl, their spirits bright.
With laughter ringing and smiles wide,
They journey together, side by side.

Through sunny days and starlit nights,
Their bond grows stronger, reaching new
heights.
In every giggle, in every cheer,
Gratitude blooms, year after year.

For in the joyful embrace they share,
Their sisterhood thrives, beyond compare.
With hearts aglow and spirits light,
They cherish the gift of love so bright.

So here's to the bond of sisters dear,
Filled with laughter, devoid of fear.
In gratitude's embrace, they shine,
Forever grateful, for this bond divine.

My brother

In the realm of dreams, where stars ignite,
A brother's love shines, ever bright.
Through trials faced and battles won,
He guides his sister, like the morning sun.

With patience as his steadfast guide,
He stands beside her, by her side.
In friendship's embrace, they walk the path,
Through laughter shared, and lessons amassed.

He teaches her to reach for the sky,
To spread her wings and learn to fly.
With every stumble, every fall,
He's there to lift her, to heed the call.

For in the tapestry of life they weave,
Their bond grows stronger, they both believe.
In the power of love and friendship's grace,
They find strength to conquer any space.

So here's to the love of brother and sister,
A bond so pure, it will never blister.
In lessons learned and dreams unfurled,
They inspire each other, to conquer the world.

Mother

In the depths of loss, when shadows loomed,
Mom's love embraced, my heart consumed.
Through shattered dreams and nights so blue,
She stayed by my side, her love true.

With a knowing touch, and words so kind,
She comforted me, a solace to find.
In moments of loneliness, she held me near,
Wiping away each lonely tear.

Even when I felt I could stand alone,
Her presence, like a beacon, brightly shone.
For she knew just what my heart yearned for,
Her love, a steady, unwavering shore.

Her life's lesson echoed, clear and bright,
"Love life, my dear, with all your might.
Embrace the unknown, don't fear the fall,
For in each moment, love conquers all."

So here's to the woman, steadfast and bold,
Whose love and wisdom, never grow old.
In loss and loneliness, in joy and strife,
Her love remains, the guiding light of life.

My love

In the quiet of night, beneath starlit skies,
I whispered my prayer, with tears in my eyes.
I asked of the heavens, with faith so pure,
For a love to cherish, forevermore.

With each breath, I surrendered my plea,
To the universe's vast and endless sea.
I sought a partner, strong and true,
A love to cherish, in all I do.

Then like a whisper, soft and clear,
Love arrived, dispelling every fear.
In the arms of destiny's sweet embrace,
I found my love, in God's own grace.

For in the dance of fate's sweet sway,
God answered my prayer, in His own way.
In the heart of love, I found my man,
A gift divine, part of His plan.

So here's to the journey, the twists and turns,
To finding love, when the soul yearns.
With faith as our guide, and love as our song,
We'll journey together, forever strong.

* 9 7 8 9 3 6 3 3 1 7 7 0 3 *